MW01288593

I AM
B.R.A.V.E

SOUL-STRONG LIVING FOR GIRLS

ASHLEY HOLT

To my beautiful and brave daughters…
Be fearless in the pursuit of what sets
your soul on fire.
-Jennifer Lee

I bow to the infinite intelligence and creative wisdom.
I bow to the divine teacher within.
- Adi Mantra

Copyright © 2018 Ashley Holt
Published in 2018 by Ashley Holt
All rights reserved. No part of this book may be reproduced or transmitted in any form or by any means, electronic or mechanical, including photocopying, recording, or by any information storage and retrieval system without permission in writing from the publisher.

Ashley Holt
www.ashleyholtbookcollection.com
www.ashleyholtbooks.com
ISBN: 978-1718919365

Acknowledgements

It is with much gratitude, I thank Lauren Helmer, my amazingly talented editor who I am privileged to also call my supporter and friend. Lauren is currently the regional editor of the South's largest digital publication, StyleBlueprint.

It is with much gratitude, I thank Dale Smith Thomas, international motivational speaker and author of "Good Morning Gorgeous", for being my light. Thank you for always believing in me, and your never-ending love and support.

It is with much gratitude I thank Gabrielle Bernstein, New York Times Bestselling author and speaker, and her books, teachings and mentorship in guiding me to shine my light. As a student of her masterclass, I also thank Rha Goddess, Lori Leyden, Jay Shetty, Jordan Bach and many others for their valuable teachings and wisdom.

Thank you, GirlSpring, a Birmingham, Alabama based nonprofit reaching girls (13-18) around the world through their online community. GirlSpring, reaching 10,000 girls monthly, provides access to reliable information, inspiring events and positive role models so girls and young women are empowered to reach their full potential. Thank you for your support and partnership. It is an honor for "I AM B.R.A.V.E" to be part of your chapter curriculum.
Visit www.GirlSpring.com on ways you can volunteer.
Empower A Girl. Change the World.

Thank you to every one who chose to pick up this book and for joining me on this journey. I love you all.

Contents

Preface

The most important lesson I have learned is that happiness starts from the inside first, then radiates outward. It is through my many stumbles and falls that I am able to write this book. I have battled low self-esteem, self-doubt and fearful ways of thinking for most of my life. I am writing every word of this to be real and authentic, and to ultimately show you the light, hope, strength and power that lies within each of you. *I Am B.R.A.V.E* is a compilation of the most effective teachings I have used to transform my fearful ways of thinking into self-love, empowerment and purpose.

My mission is to build confidence and self-esteem in girls, teens and young women through powerful positive affirmations and soul-strengthening mantras. My intention is to encourage girls and young women to discover their authentic selves and to empower them to trust the brave voice within each of their hearts. I hope to uncover the truth of what it takes to be brave in today's world.

In a society that too often extends the message that we are not enough or that, alternately, we must minimize our strengths, I hope to inspire and empower the women of tomorrow to love who they are and to honor the light they bring into this world. Our stories and our experiences are powerful. In reading parts of mine, I know you will recognize elements of your own.

It doesn't matter that as a girl growing up, I was desperate for other's approval. It doesn't matter that I suffered in silence with low self-esteem. It doesn't matter that I was a beauty pageant queen and international finalist. It doesn't matter that I was an up-and-coming Fortune 500 corporate leader. What matters is the truth that there have been many times in my life when I felt grief, rejection and failure. What matters is that I felt that I was never enough. What matters is that I escaped abuse, toxic relationships and self-attack. What matters is that I finally made the decision to choose love over fear.

I hope you will trust my ability to empower you to overcome rejection and to ignore the little voice in your head that will relentlessly tell you that you are not good enough. That voice is a liar. I hope you will allow me to empower you to stand up to that fearful voice in your head like a warrior in battle.

A warrior will win the battle of life with compassion, self-love and self-worth. I hope you will allow me to teach you how I have stood in alignment with my inner truth in the face of rejection and adversity, not just in my career, but throughout my many experiences in life. I hope you will allow me to be your guide not only in being a warrior in the situations and circumstances in your external world, but, more importantly, in being the victor in the battlefield of your own mind.

I decided to claim my power back by discovering my truth, my joy and allowing my soul to speak and to be heard. I was soaking up guidance from every self-help book, webinar or conference that crossed my path. I was so overwhelmed with the many teachings I could not hold it all in. I was catapulted onto a path I could have never imagined.

Here I am now, about to publish my fourth book and following the guidance, the power, the courage and the bravery of my heart and soul. The day I started unapologetically believing in myself is the day I decided to show up for *my* life. I decided to show up and take the responsibility to change my thoughts and to defeat the false belief systems that society projects upon us, which we knowingly — and sometimes unknowingly — accept as our truths. In that surrender, I was able to hear a louder call. "It's time for you to share this," is the voice I heard. *"I Am B.R.A.V.E – Soul-Strong Living for Girls* is the result of that powerful voice.

"A teacher of love is anyone who chooses to be."
-*A Course in Miracles.*

I believe there is an infinite force of love, compassion and truth that lives within us. We can connect to that force when we allow ourselves the freedom and ability to embody self-love and compassion from this higher perspective. When we strengthen our faith and beliefs in the presence of self-love, compassion and our own personal truths – then our lives begin to transform. We never feel the judgment, self-attack, sadness or worry. Instead, we find peace and courage, trusting our vision of self-love and self-worth. We can surrender to the voice of self-love and release false belief systems of scarcity, lack and separation. We can surrender to that voice and trust that it is powerful and guiding us to our life's highest purpose.

I believe I am no different than any other female trying to find her way in a crazy world. We all might have different circumstances, however the underlying emotions behind our situations, connect us. We all experience judgment or rejection that trigger our emotional state into fear, sadness or anxiety. It is such a gift and privilege to share these pages with you. Thank you. With gratitude, I have chosen to create this safe place to be one of transformation and empowerment. I believe by starting a conversation that matters we can help each other heal through self-love, compassion and standing in our own personal truths. This is brave. Are you ready to warrior on?

Ashley Holt

No one is you and that is your

"

power.

-Dave Grohl

Introduction

A Guide to Soul-Strong Living

Hello girls, teens and young women! I am honored that you have decided to read this book. There is nothing you will ever need in this life that is not already within you. You can do anything in this life that you so desire. You are a powerful creator. You are limitless.

Are you ready to begin the guide to soul-strong living? Are you ready to live and lead a fearless, strong and brave life? As you begin each chapter, you will be given a very important soul-strong affirmation. What is an affirmation? An affirmation is a thought. Just like we feed our body healthy food, we must feed our mind healthy thoughts. This will be the basis of this book. My mission is to give you a fun and memorable way to live life to your highest potential. You are fearless. You are strong. You are brave.

For this book, we will focus on the powerful word *BRAVE*. Every lesson, affirmation and inspiration in this book will be rooted in my acronym for the word *BRAVE*- B for beautiful, R for Ready to Rise, A for Aware of my Thoughts, V for Voice, E for Enough. These five teachings are the daily reminders I live by in order to live a positive, empowered and soul-strong life. Regardless your age, grade or walk of life, these five inspirations will guide you and give you radical confidence and limitless support.

Each chapter will also end with the *I Am B.R.A.V.E* mantra. (five minute you-tube video is also available.) A mantra is defined as an instrument or tool of the mind. Mantras are helpful in quieting the mind, while also supporting you in shifting any negative thoughts, feelings and beliefs to higher, more positive thoughts, feelings and beliefs. They are an integral part of this book.

As you repeat the I Am B.R.A.V.E mantra, it will bring your attention to your busy mind and limiting beliefs. This self-awareness is key to moving forward as a brave warrior in your life. When you are able to recognize the self-limiting beliefs, you can then intentionally transform them into your authentic statement of truth that aligns with the infinite force of love, compassion and truth that lives within us. Or simply call it your superpower.

Repeat this mantra: *I am open to receive guidance, strength and courage to step into my life's highest purpose.* I hope you will take a moment to honor your commitment to this journey.

My intention is to write in a lighthearted and loving manner all the things I wish I had known growing up. My intention is to offer you support and to be your reminder that you are loved, you are valuable and you are powerful. I want the pages of this book to be your instructional guide to living a fearless, strong and brave life. I want to make sure that all of the very important lessons I learned along the way are shared to help you along your journey in life. It is my intent to teach, guide, inspire and empower each of you throughout the pages of this book to honor yourself and honor the light that you are here to bring forth in the world.

My intention is to bring awareness to the places within your life that you are ignoring the light of who you are. The truth of who you are is always greater than the fear of who you are not. My intention is to empower you to believe in your greatness and to equip you with the necessary tools that elevate you to the next level of your highest potential. My intention is to transform your mindset from fear and limitation to one of power and limitlessness.

In the ups and downs of your journey from girlhood to womanhood, you must always remember the light and beauty of who you truly are within, so that it is never pushed aside or forgotten. You have been perfectly created with purpose and with love — in order to shine your light. You are here to light up the world. Stand unapologetically in that power.

I hope my words will fill up your heart and soul and that, with each page, you take away something very valuable. This book will be filled with positive affirmations, daily reminders, inspirational quotes, checklists, Q&As and even a place where you can journal and write your own thoughts, ideas, dreams, passions and inspirations that come to you along the way.

Get ready for a beautiful journey of self-discovery, self-love and self-worth. My goal is that by the time you finish reading this book, you are well on your way to knowing your own truth — the truth that you have the power to change the world, the truth that you are fearless, you are strong and you are brave.

I will warn you. This is not charm school, etiquette 101 or a beauty pageant. This is a book on being a warrior of your life. A warrior knows who she is and what she wants, and she goes after it with 100% of her heart. As you begin this journey, I welcome you to love, to accept, to embrace and to fully appreciate the beauty of your soul as it unfolds before you and the power of your voice as it arises within you. I hope you will make a commitment to honor this space, to make a commitment to yourself to stop hiding your magic, your beauty and all that you have to bring worth into this world.

If you can wake up every morning saying "I AM B.R.A.V.E.," then my mission will be accomplished. As you complete this book, it will be an easy way for you to remember the key steps to living a soul-strong and B.R.A.V.E life from this day forward.

"Mirrors are just glass and you are more than that."

— Zahra Kahnkan

Chapter One
I Am Beautiful

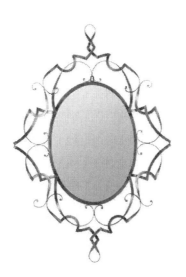

Let's start with Chapter 1 and the letter *B*. B stands for the affirmation *I Am Beautiful*. Say this three times out loud. *I Am Beautiful*. *I Am Beautiful*. *I Am Beautiful*. Say this every morning as you wake up to start your day. Repetition is key to a confident mindset and confidence is beautiful.

Do you know the power of *I AM*? Let's talk about it! "*I AM* — two of the most powerful words... for what you put after them shapes your reality," said Bevan Lee. *I AMs* will fill the pages of this book. These are affirmations or thoughts. Affirmations can be positive or negative. You can start your day saying, "*I am tired, I am bored. I am not enough,*" which are negative thoughts, or you can start your day the soul-strong way, and say, "*I am beautiful. I am confident. I am proud of who I am.*"

See the difference? Which makes you feel better? Which makes you feel ready to take on the day? Affirmations allow us to create a new belief and a new way of thinking to counteract limiting or negative thoughts. The more you allow the words to sink into your heart, the more you feel and become them. My home is filled with positive affirmations on doors, mirrors and even in the car. These constant reminders can make a big difference each day. A positive mindset is key to living a soul-strong and beautiful life.

Now let's talk about what it means to be *beautiful*. If I am going to tell you to wake up every day and say this out loud, let's be crystal-clear on its meaning. I decided to ask a few girls what defined "Beautiful" to them. Here are their answers:

Being beautiful to me is being kind, being helpful to others and being thoughtful. − Anna Cate, age 11

Beautiful isn't only about what you look like − it's about how you act and how you treat people. This defines your beauty. − Brooke, age 11

Beautiful is being yourself and not just looking beautiful, but feeling it inside and out. Everyone is beautiful in their own way. − Elli, age 11

Beautiful is having your own personality and being different from everyone else, but also being humble about it. — Lilah, age 10

It doesn't matter what you look like — it matters what's inside. — Brayden, age 7

Albert Einstein said, "If you judge a fish on its ability to climb a tree, it would spend its whole life thinking it is stupid." Our mindset is powerful. Do you compare yourself to others? Fish don't climb trees and they don't compare themselves to those animals who master this skill. They are the masters of the sea and they stand, or should I say swim, in the power of their own great ability.

Low self-esteem can be defined as a "thinking" disorder in which a girl views herself as inadequate or unlovable. Once formed, this negative viewpoint can take over her every thought, producing fear-based assumptions and self-defeating behavior. Listening, reading or writing daily positive affirmations will help you recognize your truth and stay unapologetic in it. Your truth is beautiful.

Standards of female beauty become more unrealistic every day. Dr. Gail Dines stated, "If tomorrow, women woke up and decided they really like their bodies, just think how many industries would go out of business." Research shows that media and our social networks have a profound effect on our behavior and our attitudes, including how we perceive our appearance. False messaging is everywhere. Stay in your truth, and know that confidence in who you are is beautiful.

We all have our own definition of beauty. What matters is that you stay focused on your unique abilities that you offer this world. What matters is what beautiful means to *you*. What matters is that you are happy with *you*. What matters is that you believe *you* are beautiful.

Admire the beauty in others and powerfully stand in your own greatness. Honor yourself and the greatness that you are here to bring forth into the world. Self-love and self-respect are not selfish or arrogant. It is a necessity. "It's your responsibility to share your great work with the world," said Gabrielle Bernstein, *New York Times* Bestselling author. Your great work is simply you being fearlessly and authentically you.

I want to talk for a moment about the goddess. Here is a definition of goddess.
Goddess: Beautiful, brilliant and wholesome that she is simply not like any other woman on Earth. She has many qualities like peacefulness, purity and ability.

The Collins dictionary definition of "goddess" states that in many religions, a goddess is a female being that is believed to have power over a particular part of the world or nature.

A goddess is known for her physical beauty but she is also known for her power, her inner power. For example, there is Athena, the goddess of wisdom, and Aphrodite, the goddess of love. A goddess knows her inner magic and is unapologetic in embracing it.

The goddess cherishes her inner power. How do you discover your inner power? Through your joy, you are guided to your power! For you, it might be art, science, music, dance, math, reading, writing, athletics or being in the outdoors. Tune in to your joy. Joy is beautiful. Being *you* is beautiful. Being true to your inner goddess is beautiful.

As for the definition of beautiful, what does it mean to you? Ask yourself this and make notes in the journal entry section of this chapter. Also note what brings you joy. I know when you do this step, you will connect with your inner beauty and your inner superpower. That is beautiful. *Soul-strong tip: No one is you, and that is your power.*

Recognize and honor the goddess-like strengths within you, and embrace the things that bring you joy. That is the first step in living a soul-strong and brave life. How does it feel now to know that each and every morning you will start the day by saying, "I am Beautiful"? I hope it makes you feel strong, empowered and, of course, beautiful. Knowing, claiming and stepping into your beauty is your armor in living a brave life. Step into your armor, brave warrior.

I Am B.R.A.V.E Mantra

Read or say aloud the following affirmations...

I am love.

I am light.

I am here to spread love.

I am here to transform the world.

I am here to create great change.

I am beautiful.

I am ready to rise.

I am aware of my thoughts.

I am a powerful voice.

I am enough.

I am brave.

I am [your first and last name]

Honor yourself and the love that you are here to bring forth in the world. Stand unapologetically in your power. Stand aligned in the presence of your greatness.

"I Am Beautiful" Checklist

Practice a positive mindset.

Speak, read or write positive affirmations daily.

Stay focused on your joy.

Be grateful for your unique abilities.

Stand unapologetically in your truth.

Self-love & self-respect are necessities.

Q & A

What is your definition of "beautiful"?

_____

_____

What brings you joy?

_____

_____

What is your inner superpower?

_____

_____

What is your goddess name? You are the goddess of?

_____

_____

How does it feel to say "I am beautiful"?

_____

_____

Add your own affirmations here:

_____

_____

_____

_____

Are you committed to saying them every day?

_____

_____

"I Am Beautiful" Inspirational Quotes.

Beauty isn't about having a pretty face. It's about having a pretty mind, pretty heart and pretty soul.
— Drake

Be your own kind of beautiful.
— Marilyn Monroe

Your inner beauty never needs makeup.
— Anonymous

Create a beautiful inside and you will look beautiful on the outside.
— Charles F. Glassman

Beauty is not in the face; beauty is a light in the heart.
— Kahlil Gibran

Outer beauty attracts, but inner beauty captivates.
— Kate Angell

Beauty shouldn't be about changing yourself to achieve an ideal or to be more socially acceptable. Real beauty, the interesting, truly pleasing kind, is about honoring the beauty within you and without you. It's about knowing that someone else's definition of pretty has no hold over you.
— Golda Poretsky

Journal Entry

"I'll Rise up;
I'll Rise like the

day.

I'll rise up;
I'll rise unafraid. *"*

– Andra Day

Chapter Two

I Am Ready to Rise

OK, beautiful! Are you ready to continue on the journey of a soul-strong life? Now that you have discovered all that makes you be-*you*-tiful, it's time to discover the next step of your empowerment journey. The *R* stands for the affirmation *I Am Ready to Rise*. You know the drill. Say it out loud, and repeat it three times. *I am ready to rise. I am ready to rise. I am ready to rise.*

Great job! Now let's talk about what this means. I will start by sharing with you the story of the lotus flower. I believe the lotus is a powerful example of our own ability and determination to overcome obstacles. In this chapter, the lotus represents the transformation of self-doubt to confidence, fear to fearlessness and limitation to infinite possibility.

The lotus begins its life growing from the muddy water and slowly rises toward the surface and the light. The lotus is not willing to settle for the mud. She reaches for her highest potential every day. At night, the lotus closes under the water and rises again from the mud each morning. She rises untouched and unstained by the mud, her environment and her circumstance.

Just as the lotus is determined to rise to reach the water's surface and the sunshine above, I hope you will do the same. I hope you will have high standards for your inner circle of friendships, partnerships and networks. Never settle for anyone or anything that does not believe in your special superpower, your inner truth and your limitless potential. Surround yourself with people who inspire you, touch your heart and nourish your soul. Surround yourself with people who truly desire for you to succeed on your life's beautiful journey.

Unfortunately, many are far too comfortable with mediocrity, selling themselves short, claiming their weaknesses and living life full of self-inflicted limitations. But not you, brave girl! We all get knocked down, but I hope the lotus will be your inspiration to get back up, rise up and claim your power.

Self-worth is essential for soul-strong living. The more you value yourself, the less you require validation and approval from others. Become so confident in your own self-worth, that any other opinion, judgement or criticism becomes like the muddy water to the lotus. The world is waiting on you to show your beautiful soul. Do not get stuck in the muddy water of other's opinions. Your soul is the only voice that matters. It knows the way.

The lotus never makes the choice to stay stuck in the mud. She is focused only on reaching her highest potential, which is to bloom at the top of the water's surface. She is focused on her goal and she allows nothing to get in her way. Just like the lotus, stay focused on your dreams and goals. Stay focused, dream big and reach for the stars!

There is one more lesson to be learned from the lotus. As she makes her way through the muddy water and arrives at the surface, she honors her journey. She honors herself as she blooms and absorbs the beautiful light of the morning sun. Always take time to honor yourself and your journey. Take time to honor your gifts, abilities, and your dreams. Journaling, exercise, yoga, listening to music or meditations are great ways to honor yourself, your truth, your hopes and your dreams. When you go through muddy waters, always take time to honor the infinite potential and power within you.

The journey of the lotus is a beautiful reminder for each of us. The mud symbolizes the hardships, the difficulties, the obstacles. But it also symbolizes the power of rising up and rising above. The flower, regardless of the mud, always finds its way to the light. It is in this daily growth that the lotus embodies its true beauty and purpose. What a powerful symbol of our own potential, strength and bravery.

The ability to rise is to look deep within your soul and know that your only limitations are the ones you put upon yourself. There is always a choice — the choice to live within self-made boundaries of fear and limitation or the choice to tear down the wall of fear and create the life of your dreams.

You are a powerful creator. You can choose to create sadness, weakness and loneliness or you can choose to rise to your highest potential and create empowerment, vision and strength. It is similar to changing the channel on the television. You choose one channel or you choose another. Your mind works the same way. You can choose the channel of limitation or you can choose the channel of fearlessness. You can choose the channel of weakness or you can choose the channel of greatness. You have the power to choose your thoughts. David O. McKay said, "Your thoughts are the architects of your destiny." Choose them wisely, brave girl.

Every morning as you open your eyes, I hope you will wake up ready to rise — ready to rise up and rise above. I hope every morning you will remember the determination of the lotus. I hope you remember no matter how muddy the water, you are the beautiful bloom. Keep your standards high, stay focused on your goals and live life to your highest potential. Surround yourself with people who support you and always honor the light within you.

Are you ready to rise every day? Are you ready to rise for the truth of who you are? Are you ready to rise and be unafraid to chase your biggest dreams? Are you ready to rise and believe you are capable of anything you set your mind to? Are you ready to rise and claim your divine right to a strong and limitless life? Are you ready to rise and show the world who you are and the light that lives in your heart and in your soul?

Knowing, claiming and rising to your highest potential is your shield in living a brave life. Claim your shield, and rise, brave warrior girl. Rise!

Every day I make the choice to stay focused on what I want, and if I stay focused, I will get it. — Brooke, age 11

Each day I get up, and I get ready to dance. And I dance like nobody is watching. — Anna Cate, age 11

I'm as strong as the sun. I'm as big as the sky. There is nothing that I cannot do. — Brayden, age 7

I Am B.R.A.V.E Mantra

Read or say aloud the following affirmations...

I am love.

I am light.

I am here to spread love.

I am here to transform the world.

I am here to create great change.

I am beautiful.

I am ready to rise.

I am aware of my thoughts.

I am a powerful voice.

I am enough.

I am brave.

I am [your first and last name].

Honor yourself and the love that you are here to bring forth in the world. Stand unapologetically in your power. Stand aligned in the presence of your greatness.

"I Am Ready to Rise" Checklist

Be fearless.

Have high standards for your inner circle.

Know your worth.

Be aware that others opinions are
not your truth.

Stay focused on your highest
potential.

Honor your gifts and abilities.

Prioritize you time.

Q&A:

How are you like the lotus?

_____

_____

_____

What is something in your life that represents the mud?

_____

_____

_____

How will you rise up every morning?

_____

_____

_____

Take a few moments to think about your goals and dreams. List them here.

_____

_____

_____

Describe the physical and emotional feeling of "rising up."

_____

_____

_____

"I Am Ready to Rise" Inspirational Quotes

Rise above the storm, and you will find the sunshine.
— Mario Fernandez

Everything negative- pressure, challenges — is all an opportunity for me to rise.
— Kobe Bryant

The flower that blooms in adversity is the most rare and beautiful of all.
— Mulan

We do not need magic to transform our world. We carry all of the power we need inside of ourselves already.
— J.K. Rowling

Life is either a daring adventure or nothing at all.
— Helen Keller

Do one thing every day that scares you.
— Eleanor Roosevelt

You miss 100% of the shots you don't take.
— Wayne Gretzky

Don't let anyone tell you that you can't do something, but especially not yourself. Go conquer the world. Just remember this: Why not you?
— Mindy Kaling

Journal Entry

_____

_____

_____

_____

_____

_____

_____

_____

_____

_____

_____

_____

_____

_____

_____

_____

_____

_____

_____

_____

_____

"Be a unicorn in a field of horses."

–H. B. Catherine

Chapter 3
I Am Aware of My Thoughts

Ok, fearless warriors! Now that you have mastered the first two steps in living a soul-strong life, we are on to the next step. The next daily affirmation begins with *A. A* stands for *I Am Aware of My Thoughts.* The daily affirmation is *I am aware of my thoughts. I am aware of my thoughts. I am aware of my thoughts.*

I will start this chapter with the story of the bumblebee. Did you know that aerodynamically, the bumblebee should not be able to fly? However, the bumblebee doesn't know this. The bumblebee is so confident in her purpose and ability, she spreads her wings and flies effortlessly.

I believe we can all learn a beautiful lesson of the power of our thoughts from the bumblebee. There is never a day she wakes up believing she was not meant to fly. There is never a day she wakes up and doubts her ability, her purpose or her significance in making the world a more beautiful place. Each day she wakes, spreads her wings, and flies among the flowers. Never for a moment did any other fact or opinion get in her way, slow her down or change her mind.

The Bumblebee is the perfect example of the power of our thoughts and how important it is to stay focused on our inner sense of what is true — our intuition. The bumblebee acts on her inner truth with confidence and grace. She is the perfect example of beauty, confidence and trusting our own inner power. I believe the buzzing of the bumblebee is her whisper to the world saying, "*I can, and I will.*"

I hope this story will help you be aware of your thoughts. I hope it will help you believe in yourself. I hope you will wake up every morning knowing you are beautiful, strong, brave and that you can do anything. I hope, just as the bumblebee, you will spread your wings and fly. I hope you will stay true to your inner sense of truth, the voice of your heart, and know that you are here with a purpose.

What if the bumblebee woke up every morning thinking she could not fly? The world would be missing out on all of her beauty, ability and her important role on this earth. And yes, she does have an important role. You may be thinking she is just a flying insect. But did you know that without her following her inner purpose and waking up to pollinate every day, many of our beautiful flowers and plants would become extinct. Without the bumblebee, our entire ecosystem would be completely disrupted. Every living being on this planet is here for a reason. *You* are here with great purpose.

I believe one of the biggest struggles facing girls, teens and women today is negative self-talk. You would never talk to your friends the way you talk to yourself. How many times a day do we call ourselves stupid, ugly, or talk ourselves out of an amazing opportunity? Be aware of this voice. It is a liar.

The next step is to call it out whenever you hear it. Say to this voice "I hear you, and I know you are not real." Transformation begins when you are able to hear this voice and stop it from robbing you of your potential, your truth and your power. Change the channel, and you will be catapulted into new possibilities. You will be catapulted into a life of limitless potential. This is the power of being aware of your thoughts.

The daily practice of visualizing your dreams is also a soul-strong practice. As C. Assaad said, "Close your eyes and imagine the best version of you possible. That is who you really are. Let go of any part of you that doesn't believe it." Whenever you feel negative self-talk and self-doubt creeping into your mind — remember to change the channel. You have the power to turn the channel to the best version of you.

The power of visualization is a must-have tool in your daily routine. When you hear that alarm start to buzz, instead of throwing the covers over your head, try smiling. Visualize, with your eyes still closed, the highest potential for the day. What would the perfect day look like for you? Have fun with it and know that a positive mindset is the key to an empowered life! Stay open to all the beautiful opportunities that can come your way! Take a few moments each day to imagine all the infinite possibilities of everything that can go RIGHT.

Visualizing your dreams as *already complete* can rapidly accelerate your achievement of those dreams, goals and ambitions. Your thoughts have the ability to create your reality. What are you choosing to create?

I have another story to share with you about the power of your thoughts. Do you know the fable of the chicken and the eagle? Once upon a time, there was an eagle who thought she was a chicken. When the eagle was very small, she fell from her nest. A chicken farmer found this eagle and brought her home to the farm.

The farmer raised her in a chicken coop with all the other chickens. This little eagle grew up doing all the things that chickens liked to do, believing she was a chicken. The farmer's friend would visit the farm just to see the eagle who thought she was a chicken. He could not understand why this mighty eagle, the queen of the sky, would think herself to be a chicken. The farmer would explain to his friend that this eagle had been trained to be a chicken and that the eagle believed herself to actually be a chicken.

This really bothered the farmer's friend. He knew this eagle was born an eagle and had the heart of an eagle. The friend lifted the eagle onto the fence surrounding the chicken coop and said, "Don't you know that you are an eagle? Spread your wings and fly." The eagle just looked at him confused and jumped down from the fence. The farmer then stated, "See, I told you she is a chicken."

The friend returned to the farm the next day determined to remind the chicken that she was indeed an eagle. He was determined to remind her that she was something greater than what she believed. This time, the friend placed the eagle on the roof of the barn.

"Don't you know that you are an eagle? Spread your wings and fly," he said. Once again, the eagle looked confused and jumped back down into the chicken coop.

The next day, the friend returned to the farm again. He was determined to remind the eagle that she was not a chicken. This time, he took her away from the farm. He took her out to the mountains, placed her on his arm and said, "Don't you know you are an eagle. Spread your wings and fly." At that moment, the eagle looked up into the sky, felt the warm sun on her face and stretched her massive wings. Her wings moved slowly at first, then surely and powerfully, she flew.

Shifting your thoughts can cause a miraculous change. Never forget, if you find yourself surrounded by chickens, you are an eagle. Fly, brave girl, fly! Being aware of the power of your thoughts is your sword in winning the battle over your mind, brave warrior.

I Am B.R.A.V.E Mantra

Read or say aloud the following affirmations…

I am love.

I am light.

I am here to spread love.

I am here to transform the world.

I am here to create great change.

I am beautiful.

I am ready to rise.

I am aware of my thoughts.

I am a powerful voice.

I am enough.

I am brave.

I am [your first and last name].

Honor yourself and the love that you are here to bring forth in the world. Stand unapologetically in your power. Stand aligned in the presence of your greatness.

"I Am Aware of my Thoughts" Checklist

Be aware of negative self-talk.

Visualize the best version of you.

Imagine all the infinite possibilities that can go right.

Connect to the feeling that the best version of you exists now.

See it. Believe it. Achieve it.

Change the channel when necessary.

You have the power to choose your thoughts.

Q&A

What are some of your thoughts today?

_____

_____

Are they positive thoughts or negative thoughts?

_____

_____

Which do you give more attention to?

_____

_____

Notice your thoughts when you are happy.
Notice your thoughts when you feel strong.
Notice your thoughts when you feel sad.
How can you remind yourself to change the channel of your thoughts?

_____

_____

How can you fly like the bumblebee?

_____

_____

How are you like the eagle?

_____

_____

How can you spread your wings and fly?

_____

_____

_____

_____

"I Am Aware of My Thoughts" Inspirational Quotes

One small positive thought in the morning can change your whole entire day.

Your thoughts are the architects of your destiny.
— David O. McKay

What you think, you create.
— Buddha

Your mind is a garden. Your thoughts are the seeds.
— Osho

You have the power to change your thoughts, and your thoughts have the power to change your life.
— Unknown

Identify your problems, but give your power and energy to solutions.
— Tony Robbins

Always remember you are braver than you believe. You are stronger than you seem. You are smarter than you think and twice as beautiful as you'd ever imagined.
— Rumi

If you are looking for that one person who will change your life, look into the mirror.
— Unknown

Journal Entry

_____
_____
_____
_____
_____
_____
_____
_____
_____
_____
_____
_____
_____
_____
_____
_____
_____
_____
_____
_____
_____
_____
_____
_____
_____

"The one thing that you have that nobody else has is you – your voice, your mind, your story, your vision. So, write and draw and build and play and dance and live only as you can."

– Neil Gaiman

Chapter Four

I Am A Voice

Hello, my beautiful eagle! Now that you have learned to fly, you are well on your way to a soul-strong and B.R.A.V.E life. The next affirmation begins with *V*. V represents the affirmation I Am a Voice. Repeat after me.
"I am a voice. I am a voice. I am a powerful voice. My voice matters."

Your voice is powerful. Your voice is not just how you communicate through words. Your voice can be expressed in many ways. It can be expressed through dance, art or your writing. It can be expressed through your mathematic abilities, your scientific knowledge, your athletic gifts or simply through the grace of your presence and the unfolding of your heart.

There are so many ways your voice can be expressed. My intention is that after reading this chapter, you will have discovered your unique voice — your unique gift to the world that is waiting to be uncovered, honored and celebrated.

The first step in finding your voice is to make the decision to show up. Say yes to your ability to make a difference. By picking up this book and reading the first page. You said yes. Congratulations on that step. Honor your commitment to this journey. You are brave. Mark Fisher said in *The Instant Millionaire*, "Put yourself in a position to sink or swim. Here is what you will find out. You have incredible swimming skills."

The next step is to get clear on your message. Be vulnerable. Your willingness to be imperfect is beautiful, authentic and inspiring. What are your inspirations, passions and heart's desires. You have natural abilities that bring you joy. What you love is guiding you to your message to the world. What abilities, circumstances or experiences in your life make you and your message unique and authentic to you? What you value in your life is how you decide to live your life. The amazing Rha Goddess, the soul coach behind hundreds of breakthrough changemakers and cultural visionaries says, "Live. Love. Lead."

Be willing to be imperfect. What would your life look like *without* fear? What would your life look like *without* judgment? What would your life look like *without* your own self-doubt holding you back? Fearlessly, step into your life and allow the power of your voice to lead the way.

Ignore your inner critic. Ignore self-doubt and embrace self-love. Your possibilities are unlimited. Les Brown said, "The powers that we have will never reveal themselves if we don't challenge them — if we don't put ourselves in the position where we have to use them."

Once you have decided to show up, be vulnerable and get clear on your unique message, you are ready for the next step. Have the courage to offer your gift to the world! Be B.R.A.V.E. The world has been waiting on your magic. Hide it no longer! Stop playing small with your life. Stop hiding the gift of you! Just as there are no two fingerprints alike, your voice and message is unlike any other.

Honor who you are and the authenticity of your voice, your message, your greatness. This is how you will serve the world. This is how you will create great change. Just by being you and honoring your light, you hold a powerful space for others to be inspired to do the same.

Brave girl, oh, how your voice is a treasure in every moment of every day. You share your voice with every smile, with every compliment. You share your voice every time you speak up for yourself, every time you stand up for what it is you are passionate about.

You share your voice with every hand you raise, with every audition, every team tryout. You, brave girl, claim your voice as you dream big dreams, as you wake up strong and as you pray each night. You, brave girl, claim your voice with every choice, with every thought.

In every second, in every moment, you have a voice. You leave an imprint wherever you go. What are you saying? How do you take a stand? How do you inspire and encourage others? What do you dream about, and how do you take action towards your goals every day? Your courage is your voice. Your strength is your voice. Your fearlessness is your voice. Your love and compassion for others is your voice. Your love and compassion for yourself is your voice.

To be brave is to fearlessly honor your voice. To live a soul-strong life is to use your voice. Our world has never been in more need of feminine expression. It's not who can speak the loudest. It is who can *live* the loudest. It is who can *love* the loudest. This is brave. Live your life. Love your life. It is in this, my brave eagle, you will fly. It is in this, brave girl, your voice will shine in everything you do. Knowing, claiming and using the voice of your heart is the key to victory in living a brave life.

I Am B.R.A.V.E Mantra

Read or say aloud the following affirmations...

I am love.

I am light.

I am here to spread love.

I am here to transform the world.

I am here to create great change.

I am beautiful.

I am ready to rise.

I am aware of my thoughts.

I am a powerful voice.

I am enough.

I am brave.

I am [your first and last name]

Honor yourself and the love that you are here to bring forth in the world. Stand unapologetically in your power. Stand aligned in the presence of your greatness.

"I Am A Voice" Checklist

Show up and say yes.

Be vulnerable.

Be willing to be imperfect.

Ignore your inner critic.

Get clear on your message.

Be courageous.

Be a beacon of light.

Q&A:

How do I get clear on my message? What are my inspirations and natural abilities?

_____

_____

What experiences or situations are unique to my life?

_____

_____

What do I value in my life that I would like to share?

_____

How can I share this message and my values with others?

_____

_____

How can this message impact others?

_____

_____

How can I leave my imprint every day?

_____

_____

_____

How do you feel held back in sharing your voice?

_____

"I Am A Voice" Inspirational Quotes

Be a voice, not an echo.
— Albert Einstein

Tell your truth. Find your voice. Sing your song.
— Unknown

Words mean more than what is set down on paper. It takes the human voice to infuse them with deeper meaning.
— Maya Angelou

Speak your truth, even if your voice shakes.
— Maggie Kuhn

What I know for sure is speaking your truth is the most powerful tool we have.
— Oprah

Do the universe a favor — Don't hide your magic. It's your responsibility to share your great work with the world.
— Gabrielle Bernstein

Ring the bells that still can ring. Forget your perfect offering. There is a crack in everything. That's how the light gets in.
— Leonard Cohen

Journal Entry

"You must become unshakeable in the belief that you are worthy of a big life."

— Kristin

Chapter Five
I Am Enough

B.R.A.V.E warriors, your lessons here are almost complete. You have one last affirmation in this brave journey. *E* stands for the affirmation, *I Am Enough.* Say it with confidence. *"I am enough. I am enough. Every day, I am enough."*

This, my beautiful goddesses, is the last and most powerful affirmation of all. Yes, indeed, you are enough. You are more than enough. I want to empower you now to know the power of *you* — the power of you that embodies all of the affirmations you have learned.

May you wake up every morning knowing you are enough. You are a warrior of your life. You are strength, beauty and bravery. You are beautiful. You are ready to rise. You are aware of your thoughts. You are a powerful voice. You are enough.

Along your journey, there might be days you feel alone or unsupported. This might make you feel like you are not enough or that you are doing something wrong. May you realize you are never alone. You are never alone, because you have *you*. Stand in your truth. Stand in your strength. Stand in your light. You are *you*, and that is mighty. That is powerful. That is enough! May you know that when you make decisions coming from a place of your truth, fearlessness and worthiness, all your hopes and dreams *will* come true.

Throughout your life, rejection, anger, anxiety and sadness will be revealed to you. Know that when you do face these obstacles that there is nothing wrong with you. There is nothing you need to fix. Do not minimize the importance of allowing yourself to fee*l all* of these emotions in your life. These emotions are triggers to show you an opportunity for self-love.

The greatest injustice is that of dimming your own light. Sit, honor and listen to all of your emotions and know that when you listen, it is divine guidance from the universe lighting the path to your heart's desire. The universe is saying to you "Go get it, girl."

Think of your emotions as people, as characters in your life. There is nothing wrong with you for having a variety of emotions. Sadness, anger, and frustration are all just as much as part of the journey of life as joy, love and peace. What matters is that you honor *all* of your feelings and be aware of what each one, each character in your life, is trying to tell you, and more importantly, where they are trying to guide you. You will see by feeling and recognizing what you *don't* want, it is divinely guiding you exactly to what you *do* want.

Your emotions are a compass, a map, the GPS to your highest potential. Your emotions are to be honored, not judged or dismissed. Too often, anger, frustration and sadness are judged as negative emotions — emotions that we should be ashamed of feeling. Our *natural* emotions have been given labels as good or as bad. We are taught to push away and ignore natural emotions that are meant to develop us into our highest potential.

The full spectrum of our emotions is a normal and natural part of life. *All* of our emotions have tremendous value. Many times, we feel like we are not enough or that we must be doing something wrong in our life if we experience the "so-called" bad emotions. This is not true, and it is an integral part to defeating the voice within us that tells us we are not enough.

You are human and it is part of life to feel stress, disappointment, a broken heart or feelings of failure. J.K. Rowling said, "It is impossible to live without failing at something. Unless you live so cautiously that you might as well not have lived at all — in which case, you fail by default." There is not one person on this planet that can escape these feelings. So, stop judging yourself for their appearance in your life. Here is a guide to understanding your emotions and how to move forward with each one for your highest good in each situation. I'll introduce each character, as I mentioned before. I find this is a helpful and friendly way to view our emotions as helpers, guiding us on our path.

MAIN CAST OF "FEELING" CHARACTERS & HOW THEY CAN GUIDE YOU

I am sadness. I show you the depth that you care for others and this world. When you notice me, I am trying to guide you to what it is that also brings you joy. Take time to feel what brings you happiness. That is your guidance to respond with love and compassion to yourself and to this need and then choose to go in that direction. I am sadness. Joy is my opposite, but she is my soul sister, and we are closely connected. In sad moments, say to yourself "Even though I am sad, I completely love and accept myself just as I am."

I am anxiety. When you notice me, I am trying to guide you to what it is that brings you peace. This is my alert to tell you that you are either stuck in the past or you are you worried about the future. I am anxiety. Stillness is my opposite, but she is my soul sister, and we are closely connected. Be here now and know you are exactly where you are supposed to be. Your thoughts right now are what you can control. Find gratitude in the things around you. I am your compass to gratitude and to the present moment. When you find yourself anxious, say to yourself "Even though I feel anxiety, I completely love and accept myself."

I am shame. This is your alert that you are allowing other people's opinion of who you *should be* take over *your truth.* You are human, and sometimes we make mistakes. Mistakes do not define us, they are proof that we are trying. I am your compass to be aware of where you are looking externally for approval. Pride is my opposite, but she is my soul sister, and we are closely connected. Have love and compassion for yourself during this time, and know it is your truth that matters. Everyone has an opinion — that doesn't mean you should listen. This is an opportunity for you to dig deep asking yourself, with love and compassion, what your own opinion of yourself is in that moment. It may be that you are truly proud of your actions or it may be that the answer is guiding you in the direction of taking actions toward self-growth. When you feel shame, say to yourself "Even though I am feeling shame around this situation, I completely love and accept myself."

I am guilt. Sometimes, it is hard to say no but guilt is someone else's expectation of you. Aimee Song said, "There is power in saying no. When you say no, you say yes to other opportunities." I am guilt. Honor is my opposite, but she is my soul sister, and we are closely connected. Again, this is an alert that you are allowing other people's opinion or needs to be more important than *your own*. I am a compass that your boundaries might need to be evaluated. Remember taking care of yourself and having boundaries are not selfish — they are a necessity. When guilt creeps in, say to yourself "Even though I am feeling guilt, I completely love and accept myself."

I am fear. I try to protect you from a place or situation that hurt you in the past. I love to make you aware of the worst-case scenario in *every opportunity*. My soul sister is bravery. She wouldn't exist without me, because bravery is moving forward in the direction of your true path, despite fear.

When you feel fear, this is your alert to a place in your heart that is in need of love, compassion and healing. Say thank you for the lesson, but I am safe to move forward now. Say "thank you, fear, for bringing to my attention this limiting belief. I release you now and move forward in my truth." When you feel fear, also say to yourself "Even though I feel fear in this moment, I completely love and accept myself." Fear says, I am not your biggest enemy. I am your strongest teacher of overcoming the past. "If you hear a voice within you say, 'you cannot paint,' then by all means paint, and that voice will be silenced," said Vincent van Gogh.

I am choice. You are not what the world says you are. You are the creation of your very own thoughts and choices. I am your compass to realizing your power in creating the story of your life. As Harley Davidson said, "When writing the story of your life, make sure you are the one holding the pen."

I am your heart. I have been bruised and maybe even broken. I am your guiding light. Do not be afraid of me. There is nothing that you can do that will make me not love you or see your greatness.

When you ignore any of your emotions, you are ignoring your compass and your needs and heart's desires to a joyful life. This is self-love — the knowing that you are worthy and deserving of a joyful life. Keep your emotional compass in check and in your awareness at all times. This is beautiful. This is how you rise. This is the power of your thoughts. This is how you find your voice. In *all* that you are — you are enough.

Be proud of who you are in all your many emotional states. All of these emotions are forms of love. Connect with them. Connect with yourself and how you feel. This is self-discovery. This is self-worth. This is self-love and the most important step in living a soul-strong life. This is B.R.A.V.E.

My wish for you, brave girl, is to always remember that the true meaning of this life is to stay true to who you are. Stay true to the whispers deep down in your heart and in your soul that guide you, teach you and lead you to a beautiful path of love, success and abundance. My wish for you, brave girl, is that you will never let anyone dim your light. My wish for you, brave girl, is that you will never rely on the voice of another to give you strength or to remind you of who you are and the power that lies within you.

It is time now to be a blank canvas and to paint all that you are. Paint all that brings you joy and happiness. Paint your hopes and dreams onto this canvas of life. When you make choices that lead you to more joy in your life, this is self-love. When we are full of love, we can love others more fully and authentically.

This ultimately creates great change and positive transformation throughout the world. We have been taught to sacrifice our well-being for others to a fault. We have forgotten the importance of self-love and instead have been taught to embrace self-neglect. The key to a soul-strong life is to love yourself first. You must be complete before you can serve the world to your highest potential.

As a brave warrior, sometimes you have to also surrender. My last wish is for you to surrender and allow yourself to receive the greatness of who you are. Allow yourself to create the life of your dreams. You are worthy. You are B.R.A.V.E.

I Am B.R.A.V.E Mantra

Read or say aloud the following affirmations…

I am love.

I am light.

I am here to spread love.

I am here to transform the world.

I am here to create great change.

I am beautiful.

I am ready to rise.

I am aware of my thoughts.

I am a powerful voice.

I am enough.

I am brave.

I am [your first and last name]

Honor yourself and the love that you are here to bring forth in the world. Stand unapologetically in your power. Stand aligned in the presence of your greatness.

"I Am Enough" Checklist

Stand in your truth.

You always have you.

Emotions are your GPS.

Connect with your feelings.

Always love and accept and yourself.

Be proud of you.

Surrender to your greatness.

Remember you are here to light up the world.

Q&A

If fear did not exist, I would...

_____

_____

_____

What are some things that make you feel empowered?

_____

_____

How can you shine your light in the world?

_____

_____

How can you be fearless in your life?

_____

_____

What are some of your hopes and dreams?

_____

_____

What does self-love mean to you?

_____

_____

What are some "so-called" negative emotions you feel, and what are they guiding you to realize?

_____

_____

"I Am Enough" Inspirational Quotes

True beauty is the confidence that who you are right now is more than enough.
— Unknown

Close your eyes and imagine the best version of you possible. That's who you really are. Let go of any part of you that doesn't believe it.
— C. Assaad

You lack nothing. Use what I gave you.
— The Universe

It is important to remember that we all have magic inside us.
— J.K. Rowling

You must find the place inside yourself where nothing is impossible.
— Deepak Chopra

You are better than unicorns and sparkles combined.
— Unknown

Your only limitation is the one you set up in your own mind.
— Napoleon Hill

Journal Entry

_____

_____

_____

_____

_____

_____

_____

_____

_____

_____

_____

"If your dreams don't scare you, they aren't big enough."

-Ellen Johnson Sirleaf

Chapter Six

Be Brave – Dream Big

Dream. Believe. Achieve. The dragonfly will be the inspiration for this chapter. The dragonfly symbolizes change, transformation and self-realization. Dragonflies start to grow in water and then move into the air and fly. The spirit of the dragonfly reminds us that everything is possible. We can achieve our dreams and our goals. The dragonfly is a symbol of realizing our true potential and our ability to rise up and fulfill it. It is a symbol of letting go of all that holds us back in order to achieve our dreams. The mantra of the dragonfly is "Anything is possible."

Once you have accepted and embraced the truth that you are enough, take that brave step to use your natural strengths and gifts to move forward with your dreams. I hope your quest to live the life of your dreams will not end with the last page of this book but rather be just the beginning.

A Navajo Proverb states, *"An arrow can only be shot by pulling it backward. When life is dragging you back with difficulties, it means that it's going to launch you into something great. Focus, and keep going."*

Dream Big: Creating Your Dream Board

Creating a dream board is a powerful way to stay focused on creating the life of your dreams. It is now time to know the importance of your dream board. This chapter will guide you through the steps to make the perfect one for you. When completed, you will have a powerful and inspirational everyday reminder to *dream big*, stay focused and live life to your highest potential!

A dream board is a visual way of setting goals and dreaming about your future by gathering and collecting pictures and inspiring images. You will start by gathering pretty pictures, inspirational quotes and images that describe how you like to feel — happy, motivated, empowered!

After you get your collection together, you will place all of the pictures onto a poster board or bulletin board. Get creative! Oh, and if you find yourself thinking, "This isn't possible," but it makes your heart sing, you know you should put it on there. *If your dreams don't scare you, they aren't BIG enough!*

There is no right or wrong way to create your dream board. It's all about building a visual reminder of the life journey that you have the power and ability to create. Dream it. Believe it. Achieve it!

Brave girl, thoughts are things! There is *nothing* in this physical world that was not once just a thought. Your thoughts are powerful, and you have the power to put them into action to create the life of your dreams. You are only limited by how big you dare to dream. Dream, dream bigger, then dream even bigger! See how B.R.A.V.E you can be during this process. Dream with your heart and your soul. Dream with fearlessness. Dream, knowing your worthiness. Dream big, brave girl, dream big!

Dream boards are powerful, but more importantly, *you* are powerful. Dream boards are simply a fun way to recognize the power of your intentions and the power of your ability to create anything you desire in this life. They are a powerful way to get clear on what you want so that you may take powerful action towards the life of your dreams! The power is not the dream board — the power is in your actions to make your dreams a reality.

I hope you have enjoyed this journey. You are now on your way to living a soul-strong and B.R.A.V.E life. Know that you are beautiful. Know that you are Ready to Rise. Know that you are Aware of the power of your thoughts and that thoughts are things that have the ability to manifest in your life. Know that your voice matters, and know that you are more than enough. In knowing these truths, you are the powerful creator of an amazing, beautiful and empowered life. Always remember: *You are fearless. You are strong. You are B.R.A.V.E.*

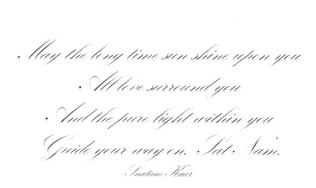

May the long time sun shine upon you
All love surround you
And the pure light within you
Guide your way on. Sat. Nam.
Suatam Kaur

I Am B.R.A.V.E Mantra

Read or say aloud the following affirmations...

I am love.

I am light.

I am here to spread love.

I am here to transform the world.

I am here to create great change.

I am beautiful.

I am ready to rise.

I am aware of my thoughts.

I am a powerful voice.

I am enough.

I am brave.

I am [your first and last name]

Honor yourself and the love that you are here to bring forth in the world. Stand unapologetically in your power. Stand aligned in the presence of your greatness.

"Dream Big" Checklist

Believe in your highest potential.

Embrace your inner truth.

Set empowering goals.

Collect inspiring quotes and images.

Get creative.

Stay focused.

Know your power.

Make your dreams a reality!

Q&A

Here are some ideas for your dream board images:

What career path interests you?

_____

_____

What is a new hobby or new activity you would like to try?

_____

_____

What are some of your favorite inspirational quotes?

_____

_____

_____

What makes you happy and you wish you could spend more time doing?

_____

_____

_____

Where would you like to travel?

_____

_____

If you could do anything knowing you could not fail what would you do?

_____

_____

"Be B.R.A.V.E — Dream Big" Inspirational Quotes

Make each day your masterpiece.
— John Wooden

The things you are passionate about are not random.
They are your calling.
— Fabienne Fredrickson

I don't have dreams. I have plans.
— Blake Atkins

Never give up on something that you can't go a day
without thinking about.
— Winston Churchill

She who dares wins.
— Eileen Gillibrand

First, think. Second, believe. And finally, dare.
— Walt Disney

Mirror, mirror on the wall, I'll always get up after I fall.
And whenever I run, walk or crawl, I'll set my goals and
achieve them all.
— Chris Butler

Shoot for the moon. Even if you miss, you will land
among the stars.
— Les Brown

Dream Big

Journal Entry

_____

_____

_____

_____

_____

_____

_____

_____

_____

_____

_____

_____

_____

_____

You Are B.R.A.V.E

You are brilliant, beautiful and bright.
Some days are hard and you'll feel the fight.
Rise, brave girl, Rise.

You are strong and brave and ready to rise.
Don't believe fear and its many lies.
Rise, brave girl, Rise.

Be aware of your thoughts and aware of your mind.
To your heart and soul, you must always be kind.
Rise, brave girl, Rise.

Use your voice and shine your light.
Remember your power with all of your might.
Rise, brave girl, Rise.

Dear brave girl, you are always enough.
Give your all when the going gets tough.
Rise, brave girl, Rise.

Life is a canvas so paint what you love.
If you spread your wings, you will rise above.
Rise, brave girl, Rise.

Dream big brave girl and create with power
And all of your fears will bow and cower.
Rise, brave girl, Rise.

Be fearless, be strong, be brave everyday
The life of your dreams is on its way.

Rise, brave girl, Rise.

—Ashley Holt

Worksheets

More Positive Thoughts and Affirmations

1. Today is going to be an amazing day.
2. It is enough to do my best.
3. Every day is a new beginning.
4. I can be anything I want to be.
5. I believe in myself and my abilities.
6. Today, I choose to be confident.
7. I can make a difference.
8. I can do anything I put my mind to.
9. I am perfect just the way I am.
10. I am an amazing person.
11. I am gorgeous.
12. I love to try new things.
13. I am a leader.
14. I stand up for what I believe in.
15. I believe in my goals and my dreams.
16. Today, I choose to think positive.
17. I have courage and confidence.
18. I deserve to be loved.
19. Great things are on their way to me.
20. I have power to make my dreams come true.
21. I have an amazing life.
22. All of my dreams are coming true.
23. I am intelligent.
24. I don't need to be perfect.
25. I love and accept all parts of myself.
26. I am unafraid.

27. I always try my best.
28. My opinions matter.
29. My words have power.
30. I have the courage to share my feelings.
31. I am deserving of great things.
32. I believe in me.
33. I am loved.
34. I am supported.
35. I honor who I am.
36. I am allowed to be different.
37. I am accepted for being my true self.
38. I am talented.
39. I think positive thoughts about myself.
40. I speak to myself with kindness.
41. I am fearless.
42. I love myself.
43. I am unique.
44. Smiling makes me feel good.
45. I am a great friend.
46. Every day, I have fun.
47. I have great ideas.
48. I love to smile.
49. I am happy.
50. I am important.
51. There is no one better to be than myself.
52. I do my best everyday
53. I am full of light and love.
54. I love to learn new things.

55. All my dreams are coming true.
56. I make new friends easily.
57. I have big dreams.
58. I shine my light every day.
59. My light is bright.
60. I believe in me.
61. I overcome challenges.
62. I am allowed to feel proud of myself.
63. I listen to my heart.
64. It's ok to be sad sometimes.
65. I am allowed to feel.
66. I respect who I am.
67. I am worthy.
68. I am special and unique.
69. I am powerful.
70. I matter.
71. I am a gift.
72. What I have to offer this world matters.
73. There is a superhero within me.
74. I love this world.
75. I love life and life loves me.

My Favorite Affirmations

1. _____

2. _____

3. _____

4. _____

5. _____

6. _____

7. _____

8. _____

9. _____

10. _____

Achieve Your Dreams Worksheet

Dream Start Date: _____

My Dream is:

_____

_____

_____

_____

Dream Completion Date: _____

Steps to Accomplish My Dream:

1. _____

   _____

2. _____

   _____

3. _____

   _____

Your Signature: _____

Positive Self Talk Worksheet

I believe one of the biggest struggles facing girls, teen and women today is negative self-talk. How many times a day do we call ourselves stupid, ugly or talk ourselves out of an amazing opportunity? Be aware of this voice. It is a liar. Transformation begins when you are able to hear this voice and stop it from robbing you of your potential, your truth and your power.

Today, I noticed my positive self-talk when:

_____

_____

_____

Today I noticed my negative self-talk when:

_____

_____

_____

How did I transform my negative self-talk to positive self-talk?

_____

_____

_____

When I am able to transform my thoughts from negative to positive, I feel: _____

I Am Brave Notes

About the Author

Ashley Holt is passionate and committed to bringing women's voices and leadership into the world. Ashley is a mother of two daughters, published author, nonprofit founder, speaker and former Mrs. Alabama. After facing divorce and becoming a single parent, Ashley reinvented her life and turned her pain into power and purpose.

Ashley's dynamic professional experience includes a successful career with a Fortune 500 company where she excelled in personal development, coaching and women's leadership roles. She is currently connecting women to their community through her impactful role with the South's largest digital publication for women.

I Am B.R.A.V.E is Ashley's fourth book. Her mission through all of her works is to build self-esteem in children through positive affirmations and soul-strong mantras. Her other works include *Miko the Perfectly Imperfect Pug, Fearless with Finley* and *Make a Wish with Marley.*

Ashley is very active in various organizations that work to empower women and girls. Through her books and public speaking, she is fulfilling her passion as a mentor with a mission to create a safe and compassionate space for women and girls to step into the authentic power of their soul. Ashley's motto — *Be fearless. Be strong. Be brave.* — describes her passion for helping others lead more powerful, fulfilling and limitless lives.

48327442R00061

Made in the USA
Columbia, SC
12 January 2019